Discovering
the Planets

Jacqueline Mitton

Troll Associates

Library of Congress Cataloging-in-Publication Data

Mitton, Jacqueline.
    Discovering the planets / by Jacqueline Mitton.
        p.   cm.—(Exploring the universe)
    Summary: Describes the sun's family of planets, moons, and comets
based on information from space probes.
    ISBN 0-8167-2130-0 (lib. bdg.)   ISBN 0-8167-2131-9 (pbk.)
    1. Planets—Juvenile literature.   2. Astronomy—Juvenile
literature.   [1. Planets.   2. Astronomy.]   I. Title.   II. Series.
    QB602.M57   1991
    523.4—dc20   90-11020

Published by Troll Associates, Mahwah, New Jersey 07430

Edited by Neil Morris
Design by Sally Boothroyd
Picture research by Veneta Bullen

Printed in the U.S.A.

10   9   8   7   6   5   4   3   2   1

All illustrations, including front cover, by Paul Doherty

Picture credits:
Akira Fujii pp 2-3, 8-9, 19, 29
Hencoup Enterprises pp 18-19
Jacqueline Mitton p 31 (bottom)
NASA back cover, pp 1, 4, 5, 6, 15, 16, 17
    (top & bottom), 20, 27, 30, 31 (top)

Front cover: Earth and the outer planets.
Title page: Saturn.
Pages 2-3: the constellation of Sagittarius.

Contents

Planet Earth   4

The Moon   6

Planets and stars   8

The solar system   10

Exploring the planets   12

Venus and Mercury   14

Mars   16

Asteroids and meteors   18

Jupiter   20

Saturn   22

Uranus, Neptune, and Pluto   24

Moons and rings   26

Comets   28

Fact file   30

Index   32

Planet Earth

If you want to know what a planet is like, you don't have to look very far. You live on one. Earth is one of the nine main planets in the solar system. Planets are huge balls of rock, metal, and gas that do not give out any light of their own.

In some ways, our planet is no different from any other. Like Mercury, Venus, or Mars, it's mainly rock with a metal core at the center. Like Venus or Mars, it's surrounded by an atmosphere of gas. And like many planets, such as Jupiter or Saturn, it has a moon.

But Earth is special among the planets. It's the only planet in our solar system with people. In fact, we can be almost certain that it is the only one with any kind of life. Animals and plants need water and air, as well as light and warmth from the Sun. Earth has plenty of all these. Three quarters of its surface is covered by oceans. From space, Earth looks deep blue with swirling patterns of white clouds.

Our planet is an active, changing world. Over millions of years, wind and rain wear down mountains, and rivers carve out valleys. Changing climates, earthquakes, and volcanic eruptions all alter the face of the Earth. So do plants and animals. Even the continents are moving – only a few inches a year, but fast enough to change the size and shape of the oceans and continents over millions of years.

◄ Earth as a crescent in the black sky over the Moon. This photograph was taken from an Apollo spacecraft in orbit around the Moon. Reflected sunlight makes the Earth shine. It is night on the dark parts of the Earth.

▲ The planet Earth as it looks from space. The swirling white patterns are clouds. The continent of Africa can be made out, with the island of Madagascar to its right. Antarctica can be seen at the bottom.

The Moon

Earth has a partner in space. Only 240,000 miles away, the Moon circles around us every month. It's a very different place from our planet. About a quarter the size of Earth, it has no water and no air. American astronauts have traveled to the Moon. They made six landings between 1969 and 1972, and brought some rocks back with them. They had to take all their air to breathe, as well as water and food. Because there is no weather, the Moon hardly changes. If you went there today, you could see the astronauts' footprints as clearly as if they had been made a few moments ago.

▲ The Moon is 2,160 miles across, and is just over a quarter as big as the Earth.

▼ An Apollo astronaut working on the Moon. The astronauts used a Lunar Roving Vehicle to travel about and explore the Moon's surface. This scene with its gray rocks is a typical moonscape.

The surface is covered with rocks and dust, and there are lots of circular hollows called craters. The biggest craters are around 150 miles across. Some have mountain peaks in the middle. The craters were made millions of years ago, when chunks of rock called meteorites crashed down from space. Many meteorites must have fallen on the Earth too, but the effects of the weather have long since worn away almost all the Earth's craters.

Look at the Moon and you can see that there are dark patches and light patches making a pattern. People thought the dark patches were seas before they knew there wasn't any water, but the name "seas" stuck. In fact, they are big areas that were swamped by floods of hot liquid rock 4,000 million years ago, not long after the Moon was formed.

▶ The craters on the Moon were made by rocks from space crashing down with tremendous force onto its surface. Moon rocks thrown up by the impact fell back to make even more craters.

Planets and stars

The Earth is a typical small, rocky planet. Among the planets traveling around the Sun there are four giants – Jupiter, Saturn, Uranus, and Neptune. These are made rather differently from the others. Each of them has a small rocky core. Surrounding it is a thick layer of ice or liquid, with gas on the very outside. No spacecraft can land on these gas giants because they don't have a surface.

All the planets are the same in one way: they don't give out any light of their own. They shine by reflecting sunlight. The Sun is different. Our Sun is a star – just like all the stars that shine in the night sky, except for the fact that it is a lot closer. A star generates huge amounts of energy at its center by a process called nuclear fusion. The energy flows out into space as light and heat. Most stars are much bigger than planets. The Sun is 109 times the size of the Earth.

▲ Planet Earth is tiny compared with the size of our nearest star, the Sun. Earth is a small rocky ball and does not give out any light of its own. The Sun is a giant globe of hot, glowing gas. It is made mainly of hydrogen. The temperature at the Sun's surface is about 9,900°F. At its center, the temperature is about 27 million °F.

► In this photograph of the night sky, Jupiter is the large bright spot near the middle. The reddish spot above it is Mars. Above Mars you can see the cluster of stars called the Pleiades or Seven Sisters.

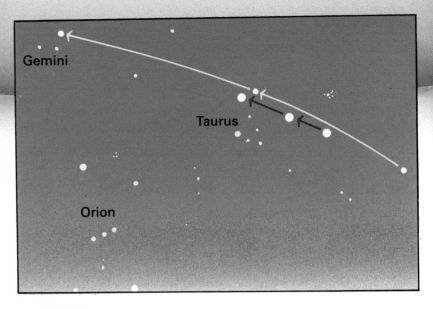

► As the planets orbit around the Sun, observers on Earth see them move slowly through the constellations. This diagram shows the paths of Jupiter (*red*) and Mars (*yellow*) through the star patterns over three months.

Only the side of a planet or moon facing the Sun is lit up. That's why we get day and night, and also why the Moon seems to change shape. At full Moon, the whole of its bright side is facing us. At crescent Moon, sunlight is falling mostly on the side facing away from the Earth.

The stars are much further away than the planets. The star nearest to us after the Sun is about 7,000 times further away than the most distant planet, Pluto. As the planets orbit around the Sun, we see them track slowly against the background star patterns. Because the stars are so far away, we don't notice any change in the patterns they make in the night sky.

9

The solar system

Have you ever wondered what keeps the planets circling around the Sun? The Sun holds on to them with a pulling force called gravity. If you could switch gravity off, the planets would speed off in a straight line into outer space.

The orbits, or paths, that the planets follow are not truly circular. They are an oval shape called an ellipse. The Sun isn't at the center of the ellipse, but over to one side, at a point called the focus. The Earth's distance from the Sun varies between 91 and 95 million miles.

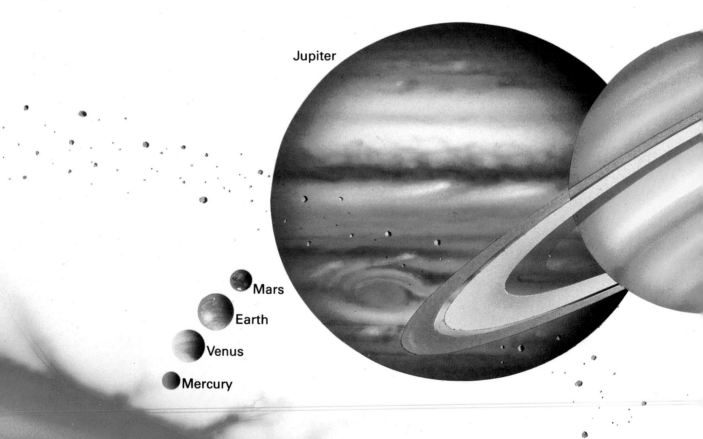

Jupiter

Mars

Earth

Venus

Mercury

Sun

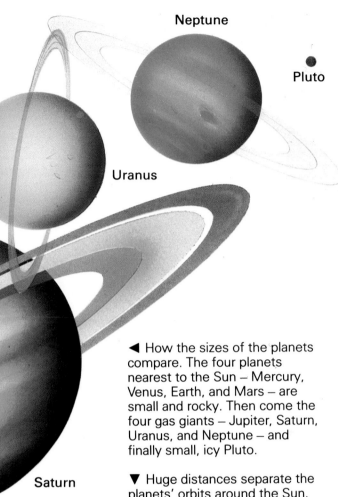

Neptune

Pluto

Uranus

Saturn

Going outward from the Sun, the nine major planets are Mercury, Venus, Earth, Mars, Jupiter, Saturn, Uranus, Neptune, and Pluto. All except Mercury and Venus have moons traveling around them, like mini solar systems. Saturn is famous for its rings, which consist of small pieces of rock in orbit, like millions of tiny moons.

In a gap between Mars and Jupiter, thousands of miniature planets orbit the Sun. These are called asteroids, or minor planets. There are also lots of small pieces of rock and specks of dust drifting in space between the planets. All this natural "junk," along with the big planets and their moons, makes up the solar system.

The planets' orbits aren't tilted at random. Nearly all of them lie in one flat disk, as if they were a set of slightly squashed rings of different sizes lying neatly inside each other on a flat table. The only odd one is the orbit of Pluto, which crosses Neptune's.

◀ How the sizes of the planets compare. The four planets nearest to the Sun – Mercury, Venus, Earth, and Mars – are small and rocky. Then come the four gas giants – Jupiter, Saturn, Uranus, and Neptune – and finally small, icy Pluto.

▼ Huge distances separate the planets' orbits around the Sun. Even the giant planets are tiny compared with the vast space between them.

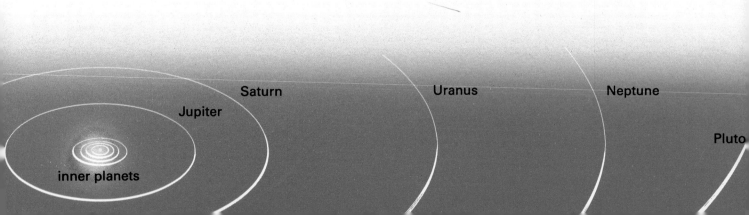

Saturn

Jupiter

Uranus

Neptune

Pluto

inner planets

Exploring the planets

How do we know what the planets are like? Astronomers have learned a lot by looking at them and photographing them through telescopes. A telescope makes a planet look much nearer. You can see patterns and details on the planets Mars, Jupiter, and Saturn through a telescope (though you should never look at the Sun through a telescope or binoculars, since you would certainly be permanently blinded). People who do astronomy for a hobby like to draw and photograph these planets. They observe the way Jupiter's clouds change and look out for dust storms on Mars.

But most of what we know about the planets comes from unmanned spacecraft equipped with television cameras and other instruments. Probes of this sort have investigated every planet except Pluto. In 1977, the United States launched the two Voyager spacecraft. Both of them flew very close to Jupiter in 1979, and near to Saturn in 1980 and 1981. After that, Voyager 2 was sent on to make a close encounter with Uranus in 1986 and with Neptune in 1989.

◄ This dome-shaped building protects the large reflecting telescope inside. The slit can be opened and closed, and the dome can turn around.

► The Voyager 2 spacecraft approaches Neptune and its biggest moon, Triton. It took twelve years to make the journey from Earth.

The Moon was the first target for spacecraft. People had always wondered what the other side of the Moon was like. From Earth, we only see one side because the Moon always keeps the same face toward us. The first pictures of the back of the Moon were taken in 1959 by the Soviet probe Luna 3. It turned out to be very much like the side we can see!

Space probes carry out different kinds of scientific experiments, as well as beaming back television pictures. Some just do a "fly-by." Others have been made to go into orbit around Venus, Mars, and the Moon, and some have landed. Computers are used to get more out of the pictures – for example, by changing the colors to bring out details that are hard to see.

13

Venus and Mercury

Have you ever spotted what looks like a really bright star in the west just after dark, or in the east just before sunrise? If so, you've probably seen Venus, the brightest of all the planets. Mercury is much harder to spot, as it's never far from the horizon. Because they are between the Sun and the Earth, Venus and Mercury go through phases (seem to change shape), just like our Moon. You need a telescope, though, to see their phases.

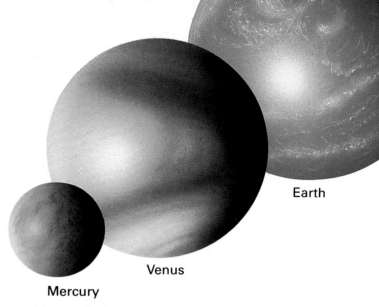

Earth

Venus

Mercury

▲ Mercury is the second smallest planet, only 3,031 miles across. Venus is slightly smaller than Earth.

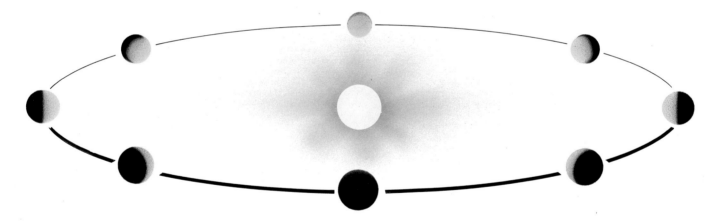

▶ From Earth, we see Venus and Mercury go through phases as they orbit the Sun. This happens because they are nearer to the Sun than Earth is.

Mercury is a small, rocky planet. With craters covering much of the surface, it looks a bit like our Moon and is not much larger. Mercury takes 59 days to spin around. On the side toward the Sun, the scorching heat is enough to melt lead during the day. At night, the temperature plunges well below freezing to −300°F, because there is no blanket of air to keep the heat in.

All you can see of Venus through a telescope are the bright silvery tops of the clouds floating in the thick atmosphere of carbon dioxide gas. Heat from the Sun gets trapped in the carbon dioxide, making Venus a planet-sized greenhouse. The surface is even hotter than Mercury's, and the atmosphere pushes down with a crushing pressure ninety times stronger than air pressure on Earth. Several spacecraft tried to land on Venus, but were destroyed. Then, in 1975, the Soviet Union sent two that were strong enough to survive there and send back pictures.

Astronomers can't see the surface of Venus directly because of the clouds. So they have to put satellites into orbit around the planet that bounce radio waves off the surface. By listening for the echoes, they have discovered mountains, plains, and craters, and built up a map of Venus.

▼ This is what astronomers think Venus may be like beneath its thick layers of clouds. The surface temperature is about 900°F, and the atmosphere weighs down with a huge pressure.

Mars

Through a telescope, Mars looks like a rusty-orange disk with some darker patches on it and white ice caps at the north and south poles. The year on Mars is twice as long as ours but, as on Earth, there are seasons. The ice caps get bigger and smaller, and some of the markings change too.

For a long time, people imagined that there might be life on Mars. But two American spacecraft, Viking 1 and 2, landed there in 1976 and found no sign of life. Many television

▲ Mars' diameter is just over half that of Earth. Like Earth, Mars has ice caps at its north and south poles.

pictures were sent back from the surface and from spacecraft that stayed in orbit to survey the whole planet.

◄ The view from the Viking 1 spacecraft after it landed on the surface of Mars in 1976. Mars is sometimes called the Red Planet because the soil and rocks are a reddish color. This red color is caused by iron oxide, the chemical name for rust. Various-sized rocks litter the Martian landscape. The two Viking spacecraft photographed the landscape and recorded the weather, winds, and temperature. They found no signs of life.

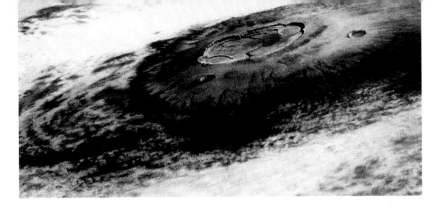

► The largest of Mars' four giant volcanoes, Olympus Mons. It is 370 miles across and 17 miles high. None of the Martian volcanoes has erupted for millions of years.

▼ Mars seen from about 190,000 miles away, in a photograph taken by the Viking 1 spacecraft.

There is no running water on Mars, and everywhere is like a desert. Dried-up river beds show that Mars did have water long ago, but it must be millions of years since there was last any rain.

There is a thin atmosphere of carbon dioxide, and patches of clouds and mist sometimes form. Even the polar caps are mostly just a frost of solid carbon dioxide (sometimes called "dry ice"). High winds blow the dust around, making the sky look pink. Occasionally, all of Mars is engulfed in a massive dust storm.

The surface is pitted with lots of craters, but the most dramatic features are the spectacular Mariner Valley and several enormous extinct volcanoes. The Mariner Valley is three or four times deeper than the Grand Canyon in Arizona, and long enough to stretch halfway across the United States. The largest volcano, called Olympus Mons, is nearly three times as tall as Mount Everest, the highest mountain on Earth.

Mars has two very small moons.

Asteroids and meteors

On New Year's Day, 1801, a new planet was discovered in orbit between Mars and Jupiter. It was named Ceres but turned out to be tiny – less than 600 miles across. Ever since then, astronomers have been discovering more and more of these mini-planets. Known as asteroids or minor planets, most of them circle the Sun in a band called the asteroid belt, though some have very long, elliptical orbits that bring them close to the Sun or the Earth. Astronomers know of more than 3,000 asteroids, but you usually need a telescope to pick out even the brightest.

There are lots of pieces of rock and specks of dust flying around in space between the planets. Some of them collide with the Earth, but we do not notice anything because they burn up high in the atmosphere. On clear, dark nights, you can often see the streaks of light they make. They are called meteors, or "shooting stars."

Sometimes a larger rock falls all the way to the ground without burning up. These stones from the sky are known as meteorites. When a meteorite falls, it makes a brilliant trail in the sky called a fireball.

▲ The four largest asteroids – Ceres, Vesta, Pallas, and Juno – compared with the size of our Moon.

Scientists can tell that certain rocks are meteorites, even if nobody saw them fall. The largest known meteorite weighs 60 tons and still lies where it fell long ago in southern Africa. There's a 30-ton meteorite in the American Museum of Natural History in New York. It was found in Greenland by the American explorer Robert Peary.

When the Earth collides with a swarm of meteors in space, they seem to rain down from one patch of sky. Meteor showers tend to happen on the same dates each year. During the most spectacular ones, a meteor may be seen every minute.

▲ A bright meteor trail or "shooting star." The trail lasts for a few seconds.

◄ This famous meteorite crater in Arizona, USA, is 4,150 feet across and 575 feet deep. It was made when a large iron meteorite fell at least 20,000 years ago.

▼ This is what a stony meteorite (*in front*) and an iron meteorite (*behind*) look like when they are sliced through.

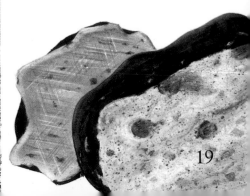

19

Jupiter

Swirling, colored cloud tops are all anyone can ever see of the gas giant Jupiter. Through a small telescope, it appears as a yellowish disk with a couple of darker bands across it. You would also see some of Jupiter's four biggest moons, as small points of light near the planet. These moons are sometimes called the Galilean moons because the Italian astronomer Galileo discovered them in 1610. Their names are Io, Europa, Callisto, and Ganymede. If you've got binoculars or a small telescope, it's not difficult to follow them from night to night as they move in orbit around Jupiter.

▲ This close-up photograph of part of Jupiter was taken by a Voyager spacecraft. It shows the Great Red Spot, Jupiter's most famous cloud feature.

Jupiter

The best pictures of Jupiter and its moons came from the Voyager space probes. From close up, they beamed pictures to Earth of moving patterns in the planet's cloud belts. The most famous cloud feature on Jupiter is a huge oval called the Great Red Spot. It's several times bigger than the Earth, so it's easily seen through a telescope. Astronomers have known about it for more than 300 years.

We know that Jupiter has at least 16 moons. Ganymede is larger than the planet Mercury. The smallest of them, Leda, is only 10 miles across. The Voyager pictures show that each of Jupiter's moons is different; though, like our Moon, most have craters. The most unusual one is Io. The Voyager probes saw eight active volcanoes showering plumes of sulfur over Io's surface. They also found a very thin ring around Jupiter, too faint to be seen from Earth.

▼ Jupiter and its four largest moons, Io, Europa, Ganymede, and Callisto — compared for size. Io is slightly bigger than our Moon, and Europa is a bit smaller. Ganymede is slightly bigger than the planet Mercury, and Callisto is a little smaller. Each moon looks quite different. Io is a mixture of red, yellow, orange, black, and white. These colors come from sulfur erupted from Io's active volcanoes. Europa has a bright surface, made mainly of ice. Ganymede looks rather patchy, with bright marks where meteorites have made craters in the icy surface. Callisto's darker surface is probably a mixture of rocky material and ice. It is covered all over with a huge number of craters.

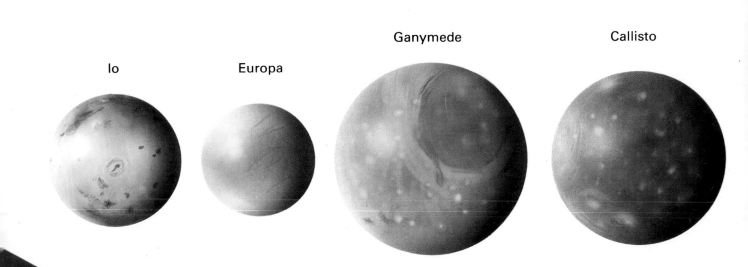

Io   Europa   Ganymede   Callisto

Saturn

Saturn's amazing rings make it perhaps the most beautiful of all the planets. Astronomers have known about the rings since they first had telescopes to turn on the sky.

Saturn itself is a bit dull. It's rather like a smaller version of Jupiter, but it is not so colorful. The cloud belts are hazy, and there isn't nearly as much detail to be seen. The planet is made mainly of the gases hydrogen and helium. A typical chunk of Saturn weighs so little it would float in water.

The rings actually consist of countless small pieces of rock coated with ice, some perhaps no bigger than grains of dust. Each piece travels around Saturn in its own orbit, like a miniature moon. The rings are probably less than 200 yards thick.

Sometimes, the view we get of Saturn from Earth is with the rings edge-on. When that happens, the rings disappear from sight for a few days. At other times, the rings are tipped toward us so we can see the dark gaps in them. The Voyager close-ups showed that each ring is made of hundreds of narrow ringlets.

As well as the rings, Saturn has at least 20 moons, though many of them are tiny. Titan, the biggest by far, is the second largest moon in the solar system. It is the only moon in the solar system with a real atmosphere, consisting mainly of nitrogen gas. Because thick reddish clouds fill the atmosphere, the Voyager spacecraft couldn't see what Titan's surface is like.

▲ Saturn and some of its moons, compared with the Earth for size. The volume of Saturn is great enough to swallow 744 Earths.

23

Uranus, Neptune, and Pluto

To see the planets at the edge of the solar system you would need a fairly powerful telescope. Uranus and Neptune are both giant planets, about four times the size of the Earth, but they look quite different. In pictures from Voyager 2, hardly any features could be seen on Uranus – just faint, hazy bands. In contrast, Neptune has distinct bands and several dark spots, including a huge one with white, wispy clouds over it.

▶ Uranus and four of its moons, compared with the Earth for size.

William Herschel, who later became a famous astronomer, discovered Uranus by accident in 1781. After a few years, observers noticed that the new planet wasn't keeping to the path they expected. They thought that the gravity of an unknown planet must be pulling Uranus off course. It turned out that this explanation was true, and Neptune was found in 1846. Convinced that there was still another planet to be discovered, astronomers kept searching. Eventually, Pluto was spotted in 1930.

▲ Neptune and its largest moon, Triton. At the top right is Pluto, with its moon, Charon.

Uranus has at least 15 moons and 11 thin rings. Nine of the rings were discovered in 1977 when Uranus passed in front of a star. The rings made the starlight flicker as if it were being turned on and off, but they are much too faint to be seen from Earth. In 1986, Voyager 2 photographed the rings and some of Uranus' moons, including ten tiny ones that had never been seen before.

Three years later, in 1989, Voyager 2 flew past Neptune. We already knew about two of Neptune's moons, Triton and Nereid. But Voyager discovered six more moons and revealed that Neptune has three rings around it.

Pluto is about the size of our Moon. In 1978, photographs taken through a large telescope showed up Pluto's own moon, Charon. Because Pluto is so far away, it receives little heat from the Sun. The temperature of this frozen world must be around −400°F.

Moons and rings

Now that spacecraft have traveled to most of the planets, we've got good pictures of many of their moons. It's interesting to compare them. One thing we've found out is that no two moons are quite the same.

Nearly all of them have craters where meteors crashed down long ago. Then there are ridges, cracks, and patches of color. Astronomers try to work out what the moons are made of and how they have changed since they formed from a giant cloud of gas, along with the Sun, about 4,600 million years ago.

The big moons, like ours, are more or less ball-shaped. They are made of rock, or a mixture of rock and ice. The huge number of tiny moons around Jupiter, Saturn, and Uranus, as well as Mars' two moons, are mostly potato-shaped pieces of rock.

We also know now that four planets, Jupiter, Saturn, Uranus, and Neptune, have rings. But only Saturn's can be seen directly from Earth.

Hyperion (Saturn)

Nereid (Neptune)

Phoebe (Saturn)

Amalthea (Jupiter)

Moon (Earth)

Mimas (Saturn)

Phobos (Mars)

Deimos (Mars)

Miranda (Uranus)

26

◄ Some of the smaller moons of the solar system, compared with our Moon for size.

► A close-up of Saturn's rings. The colors have been exaggerated by a computer, to show where the icy particles making up the rings have different types of materials in them.

Comets

It's not often people get the chance to see a bright comet. When one appears, it looks like a star with a long misty tail trailing across the sky. It stays visible in the sky for several weeks, getting gradually brighter, then fading again. Using telescopes, astronomers detect about 20 different comets every year, but most of them are quite faint.

Astronomers think that comets were probably formed about 4,600 million years ago, at the same time as the rest of the solar system, far out at its most distant edge. There may be a cloud of them scattered around the solar system, too far away to be seen from Earth.

Comets orbit the Sun and some come back regularly, so we can keep track of them. Halley's Comet is the most famous. It's seen every 76 years. But most comets have long stretched-out orbits that take them far out into space. It takes thousands of years for them to get back near the Earth, and some of them may never return.

Comets can be truly enormous. The fuzzy part around the head, called the coma, may be hundreds of thousands of miles across, and the tail can stretch for many millions of miles. The coma and the tail are made of thin gas that shines as it reflects sunlight. They grow as the comet gets near to the Sun. At the center of the comet's head is a very small solid part, called the nucleus.

▲ Comet Bennett. Its long tail is clearly visible.

◄ This spacecraft, called Giotto, flew to within 380 miles of the rocky nucleus of Halley's Comet in 1986. It found that the nucleus is 9 miles long and 5 miles wide, and sent back photographs showing bright jets of gas streaming out from the nucleus.

Thanks to space probes, scientists have learned an enormous amount about the Sun's family of planets, moons, and comets. We can be fairly sure there are no more major planets to be discovered in our solar system. But one day astronomers may prove that there are planets circling around some distant stars.

Fact file

The planets: facts and figures

	diameter	distance from Sun	spin time	orbit time	moons
Mercury	3,031	36	59	0.2	0
Venus	7,521	67	243	0.6	0
Earth	7,928	93	1	1	1
Mars	4,217	142	1	1.9	2
Jupiter	88,732	483	0.4	11.9	16+
Saturn	74,567	885	0.4	29.5	20+
Uranus	31,567	1,781	0.7	84.0	15+
Neptune	30,200	2,789	0.8	164.8	8
Pluto	1,460	3,670	6.4	247.7	1

diameter: at the planet's equator, in miles
distance from Sun: average distance, in millions of miles
spin time: period of rotation, in days
orbit time: period of orbit around the Sun, in years
moons: number of moons or satellites

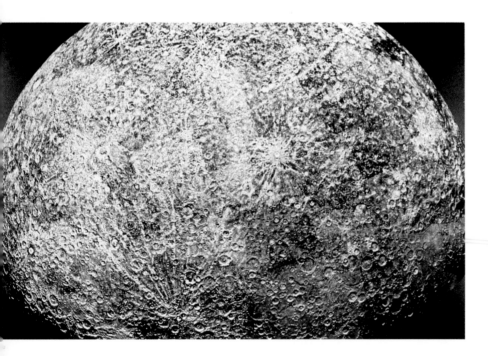

The size of the Sun
The Sun is much bigger than any of the planets. Its diameter is 865,000 miles, which is 109 times greater than the Earth's. It would take 1,300,000 Earths to make a ball as large as the Sun.

The largest and smallest planets
Jupiter, the largest planet, is big enough to hold 1,318 Earths. Pluto is the smallest planet, was the last to be discovered, and gets furthest from the Sun. Its diameter is less than that of the Moon. Pluto's orbit is very oval. Its distance from the Sun varies between 2,760 and 4,591 million miles.

Where the planets came from
The Sun and the planets were formed about 4,600 million years ago from a cloud of dust and gas in space.

The largest moon
Ganymede, one of Jupiter's moons, is the largest in the solar system. Its diameter is 3,270 miles, which is greater than Mercury's. Saturn's moon Titan is a close second at 3,200 miles.

◄ Mercury is a small, rocky planet.

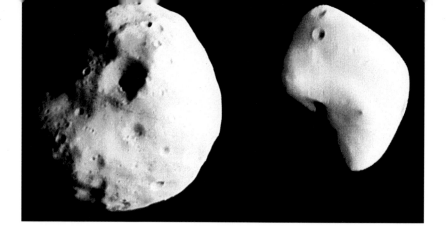

The smallest moons

The smallest known moon belongs to Mars. Deimos is not a perfect ball-shape, but measures between 7 and 9 miles. Mars' other moon, Phobos, is a little larger. Jupiter also has several tiny moons ranging between 10 and 16 miles. Saturn and Uranus each have several moons only a little larger.

▲ The Martian moons, Phobos (*left*) and Deimos (*right*).

The Earth's satellite

The Moon has a diameter of 2,160 miles, just over a quarter as big as the Earth. On the average, it is 238,000 miles from Earth. The Moon takes 27.3 days to orbit the Earth.

The largest lunar crater

At 183 miles across, a crater called Bailly is the largest on the Moon.

Traveling light

The Sun's light reaches the Earth in just over 8 minutes. Light from the next nearest star, Proxima Centauri, takes more than 4 years to reach Earth.

Asteroids

The largest is Ceres, with a diameter of 584 miles. The smallest known asteroids are only a third of a mile across.

The brightest asteroid

Vesta is the only asteroid that can sometimes be seen without the help of a telescope. The darkest known asteroid, Arethusa, has a surface as black as coal.

Closest encounter

The closest known approach to the Earth of an asteroid was in 1937 when Hermes came within 500,000 miles.

Danger from meteorites?

There is no record of anyone ever being killed or seriously hurt by a falling meteorite. In 1954, a woman in Alaska, USA, suffered a bruised arm when a meteorite fell through the roof of her house.

Comet tails

A comet seen in 1843 had a tail 205 million miles long, which is further than the distance between the Sun and Mars. A comet discovered in 1743 grew six separate tails – the most ever seen on one comet.

◄ This small meteorite weighs 535 pounds.

Index

Africa 5, 19
Alaska 31
Amalthea 26
Antarctica 5
Apollo spacecraft 5, 6
Arethusa 31
asteroids 11, 18, 31
astronauts 6
atmosphere 4, 15, 17, 18, 23

Bailly crater 31
binoculars 12, 20

Callisto 20, 21
carbon dioxide 15, 17
Ceres 18, 31
Charon 25
coma 28
Comet Bennett 29
comets 28, 29, 31
computers 13, 27
constellations 9
continents 4, 5
craters 7, 15, 17, 18, 19, 21, 26, 31

Deimos 26, 31
dry ice 17
dust storms 12, 17

Earth 4, 5, 6, 7, 8, 11, 12, 13, 14, 16,
    17, 18, 19, 23, 26, 28, 30, 31
earthquakes 4
ellipse 10
Europa 20, 21

fireball 18
fly-by 13
focus 10

Galileo 20
Ganymede 20, 21, 30
gas giants 8, 11, 20
Giotto spacecraft 28, 29
Grand Canyon 17
gravity 10, 24
Great Red Spot 20, 21
Greenland 19

Halley's Comet 28, 29
helium 22
Hermes 31
Herschel, William 24
hydrogen 8, 22
Hyperion 26

ice caps 16
Io 20, 21
iron oxide 16

Juno 18
Jupiter 4, 8, 9, 10, 11, 12, 18, 20,
    21, 22, 26, 30, 31

Leda 21
Luna spacecraft 13
Lunar Roving Vehicle 6

Madagascar 5
Mariner Valley 17
Mars 4, 8, 9, 10, 11, 12, 13, 16, 17,
    18, 26, 30, 31
Mercury 4, 10, 11, 14, 15, 21, 30
meteorites 7, 18, 19, 21, 31
meteors 18, 19, 26
Mimas 26
Miranda 26
Moon 4, 5, 6, 7, 9, 13, 14, 26, 27,
    31
moons 4, 9, 11, 20, 21, 23, 24, 25,
    26, 27, 29, 30, 31
moonscape 6
mountains 4, 7, 15
Mount Everest 17

Neptune 8, 11, 12, 24, 25, 26, 30
Nereid 25, 26
nitrogen 23
nuclear fusion 8
nucleus 28, 29

oceans 4
Olympus Mons 17
orbits 10, 11, 18, 22, 30, 31
orbit time 30

Pallas 18
Peary, Robert 19
phases 14
Phobos 26, 31
Phoebe 26
plains 15
Pleiades 8
Pluto 9, 11, 12, 24, 25, 30
probes 12, 13, 21, 29
Proxima Centauri 31

radio waves 15
Red Planet 26
rings 11, 21, 22, 23, 25, 26, 27
rust 16

satellites 15, 30, 31
Saturn 4, 8, 11, 12, 22, 23, 26, 27,
    30, 31
"seas" 7
seasons 16
Seven Sisters 8
shooting stars 18, 19
solar system 4, 10, 11, 23, 24, 28,
    29, 30
spin time 30
stars 8, 9, 14, 25, 28, 29, 31
sulfur 21
Sun 4, 8, 9, 10, 11, 12, 14, 15, 18,
    25, 26, 28, 29, 30, 31

tail 28, 31
telescope 12, 25
Titan 23, 30
Triton 12, 13, 25

Uranus 8, 11, 12, 24, 25, 26, 30, 31

Venus 4, 10, 11, 13, 14, 15, 30
Vesta 18, 31
Viking spacecraft 16, 17
volcano 4, 17, 21
Voyager spacecraft 12, 13, 20, 21,
    23, 24, 25

weather 6, 7, 16, 17